LAKE DISAPPOINTMENT

Lachlan Philpott
& Luke Mullins

Currency Press,
Sydney

CURRENCY PLAYS

First published in 2017
by Currency Press Pty Ltd,
PO Box 2287, Strawberry Hills, NSW, 2012, Australia
enquiries@currency.com.au
www.currency.com.au

Cataloguing-in-publication data for this title is available from the National
Library of Australia website: www.nla.gov.au

Typeset by Dean Nottle for Currency Press.
Cover design: Studio Emma.
Cover image: Luke Mullins. Photo by James Brown.

Currency Press acknowledges the Traditional Owners of the Country on which
we live and work. We pay our respects to all Aboriginal and Torres Strait
Islander Elders, past and present.

Contents

Australian Government | Australia Council for the Arts

Publication of this title was assisted by the Commonwealth Government through the Australia Council, its arts funding and advisory body.

LUKE MULLINS is an award-winning actor, director and writer. He has performed with independent and mainstream theatre companies, including Belvoir, Sydney Theatre Company, Melbourne Theatre Company and Malthouse Theatre. Luke's excellence has been recognised with several awards such as the George Fairfax, Green Room, Sydney Theatre and Helpmann Awards. Some of his most prominent productions thus far include *The Glass Menagerie*, *Angels in America*, *Small and Tired* (Belvoir), *Waiting for Godot* (STC), *Rosencrantz and Guildenstern Are Dead* (Old Vic, UK), *Thom Pain* and *The Eisteddfod*.

LACHLAN PHILPOTT is a Sydney-based writer, dramaturg, teacher and dog person. As a writer he has worked with many theatre and arts companies in Australia, England, France, Kenya, Scotland and the USA. Lachlan has a long-term creative collaboration with director/academic Dr Alyson Campbell who has directed the premieres of several of his new works.

Lachlan's plays include *Bison, Bustown, Catapult, Colder* (winner of the R.E Ross Trust Award), *In 3D, Lake Disappointment, Michael Swordfish, M.ROCK, promiscuous/cites, Run Rhianna Run!, Silent Disco* (winner of the Griffin Award for Outstanding New Australian play, the GAP Competition Aurora Theatre Co. USA, the best stage play, Australian Writers' Guild Awards), *The Chosen, Truck Stop* (winner of best play, young audiences Australian Writers' Guild Awards), *The Trouble with Harry* and *Walter*.

Lachlan was awarded an Australia Council Cultural Leadership grant to study new play development models in several countries and was named the inaugural Australian Professional Playwright Fulbright Scholar in 2014/15. Lachlan was Chair of the Australian Writers' Guild Playwrights' Committee between 2012 and 2015.

INTRODUCTION

This play sneaks up on you. After the mysterious opening image—a man standing in a lake with his arms stretched wide—we quickly think we know what we are watching. He is the double of a famous film star, employed to stand in for 'Kane' for the scenes that are beneath the real actor's attention. Here they are doing a helicopter shot.

As we see him go through a series of increasingly trivial activities—walking down a street and knocking on a door, moving a coffee cup—we gradually realise the extent of his narcissism. Here is a man who seems to have no idea of how unimportant he is. All his 'scenes' are extreme long shots or close-ups of his hands or the back of his head—in all of them, it won't matter that he is not Kane.

Other than his precise recounting of the technical details of his specific tasks, he seems to have very little idea of what is going on. He tells us that he never reads the script and we can see that he has no sense of what the film is about. He doesn't know the whereabouts of the real Kane, whom we later discover has been in town all along. He doesn't recognise the distinctive-looking Oscar-winning actor Linda Hunt, thinking she is an employee of the place he is staying. As he stands there in the lake, or sits in the restaurant moving his coffee cup, he, at first apparently idly, reminisces about his life: missing out on the Wobble Bobble ad that might have set up his career, starting out as a hand-actor (he is proud of his hands) before becoming Kane's double in the series of movies that made Kane's name but not his. He has no name of his own. He is simply the Double.

All this is very funny and increasingly poignant. There is nothing very likeable about him. As a boy he tried to befriend James, who got the part in the ad, but only in an attempt to get into an ad himself. He sneakily killed James' favourite fish, something James seems to have realised the next morning. He is obsessed with being 'recognised', with how many seconds of screen time bits of his body will get, and with winning an award at the annual Body Double Convention.

As his story develops, however, we gradually come to understand his profound loneliness. He seems to have no-one in his life other than his agent Gina and the absent Kane. In the otherwise comic list of his own disappointments he reveals that he was an only child. He has alienated his only potential childhood friend. He keeps sending messages to Kane and never gets a reply. He invests apparently banal remarks with great significance. Linda tells him that he has a stillness, and he is proud of that—later the second-unit director asks him to shake more, in his hand-acting. Linda asks him, 'What do you want?', and he absurdly takes that as a profound question about his identity. Above all, in his obsession with being Kane (he refers often to 'our' character and 'our' film), he is mystified by Kane's ability to act out inner thoughts, which is ironic because we have been inferring his inner thoughts all along, from the subtext of his rambling.

And so we come to sympathise with him, despite all the unattractive aspects of his personality. The mix of humour and pathos is very pointed in his account of the Body Double Awards night in Atlanta:

> In Atlanta it's just us. We call each other by our actors' names.
> Nice to see you, Brad. Jennifer ... Jennifer.
> It's the only time we can really be ourselves.
> No stand-ins, no stunt doubles, 'cause they all come and go. In
> Atlanta, it's just us body doubles because we are the constants.
> You're only allowed to come to the convention if you're working.
> Poor Heath. (p.16)

It's very funny and very sad. You can only be yourself by being someone else.

Then, in the bathroom scene (Scene Six), the play sneaks up on us again by suddenly moving into an entirely different world. There have been hints of anorexia in the Double's constant dieting and attempts to buff up, but these may be explained by his need to match the requirements of Kane's roles. He was particularly good at thinning down for the concentration camp scene in an earlier movie, better than Kane. ('I had to start eating more because I was too good.' p.2) The bathroom scene might have been his big break, because all of his body, at least from the neck down, might have made it onto the screen. He never explains why the director so angrily rejects the shots—he probably has no idea—but we think that it might be because his body has shrivelled with his dieting. Or perhaps this is, at least metaphorically, an AIDS play. (For people who remember the first onslaught of that terrible disease the imagery evokes the wasting bodies of the sufferers.) Or perhaps, we think by the end of the scene, because he has ceased to exist entirely. He cannot see his reflection in the steamy mirror.

During and after that scene the Double's reality fragments entirely. There is the story of the boy, the only other person in his world. The boy may be the one who stood at the edge of the lake in the first scene. By now he has become either an imaginary childhood friend or perhaps himself—another double.

Our poor lonely man is then caught up in the grotesque carnival of the Flapping Day scene and the end-of-shoot party. The 'reality' of the film set has been swept away. Kane, who has never appeared, has gone. When the Double gets back up the mountain the town has disappeared, packed up like so many discarded flats and props.

This work is the result of a brilliant collaboration between Luke Mullins and Lachlan Philpott. Mullins played the Double in the 2016 production directed by Janice Muller at Carriageworks, Sydney, where it was performed in one of the largest spaces of that venue.

After Scene Six the curtains that had been enclosing the stage disappeared and a great void was revealed, into which this nebulous character walked away and all but vanished, like an actor in extreme long shot, or like a man who never, in his own right, really existed.

John McCallum
Sydney, 2017

John McCallum is a theatre reviewer for *The Australian*.

ACKNOWLEDGMENTS

This work received support through many stages of writing and development. We would like to thank: Bell Shakespeare for commissioning it through their Minds Eye program (especially Pete Evans and Gill Perkins and for supporting the ongoing development). Alyson Campbell and Steve Toulmin for their artistic input at this early stage. Lyn Wallis and Tahni Froudist at HotHouse and Tim Roseman and Playwriting Australia for supporting development vital to this new work.

Special thanks to Lisa Ffrench and Lisa Havilah at Carriageworks for seeing a place for the premiere in one of Sydney's best and largest spaces. Like all the best theatre, the making of this piece was a true collaboration and the artists who worked to create the premiere of *Lake Disappointment* extended themselves far beyond their acknowledged disciplines: Matt Cox, Michael Hankin, James Brown and the brilliant Janice Muller.

Lake Disappointment was first produced at Carriageworks, Sydney, on 20 April 2016, with the following cast:

DOUBLE   Luke Mullins

Director, Janice Muller
Set and Costume Designer, Michael Hankin
Set and Costume Assistant Designer, Charlie Davis
Lighting Designer, Matt Cox
Composer and Sound Designer, James Brown
Stage Manager, Jennifer Parsonage
Production Manager, Cat Studley

PRODUCTION NOTE

The only character on stage is a film DOUBLE.

The scenes take place on a film shoot, mostly while the DOUBLE is working.

Stage directions for action are suggestions only.

The DOUBLE usually addresses the audience, but sometimes he is in conversation with the film crew.

SCENE ONE

SC. 113. EXT. LAKE. EARLY MORNING.

There was this girl in my year at school. Everyone called her The Rabbit. She twitched. Did this thing with her nose. What was her name?

Rebecca?

Rachel?

When she stopped being called——and started being called The Rabbit.

Ruby?

Ruth?

Rochelle? I can't even remember her face. Just …

Oh, look! A fish!

I went fishing once when I was a kid. Didn't catch anything, but the guy next to us kept pulling them in and grinning away, standing on their faces and ripping out the hooks. Then he cast his line the wrong way. The hook curled back into his face, kind of tore his nostril, so much blood. He probably has uneven nostrils now.

Looks cold and it is.

I'm standing in the lake but that's not all I'm doing.

People walking down here with their rods. Past the church and the diner and the row of houses, the big plastic fish with the sign in its mouth. Fucking fishing. Watch your faces. Come and eat my worm. Come and eat my worm. Oh, you ate the worm, I'll put another one on. Come and eat my worm.

This town's a bit weird.

But it's only five weeks. Five weeks. Thirty-five days. And then Paris. Easy. Paris.

Bonjour.

Je m'appelle.

Baguette.

Helicopter for the aerial shot. It'll actually be me you see in the film.

Rhonda? Rhoda? Rabbit … rabbit. Dressed as a rabbit for the Easter bonnet parade. Rabbit who?

Kane'll be on set tomorrow. Looking forward to seeing him. Haven't seen him since we shot *Path of the Willing.* Got a picture in my mind how he'll be. His sixpack. The little mole on his neck. Can't wait to see how he's looking.

Kane has to beef up for the Paris role. We both do. They want us to be really big for the fight scenes—so more protein, less carbs. We both have a bit of work to do to get the look right—but I think I'm going to get there.

When we did the concentration camp; that was hard. Took him forever to get all the ribs to show. I beat him. Easy. He made a good Jew but I was better, even he said that. But we both made good Jews. I had to start eating more because I was too good.

He should've won the Oscar, should have been a shoo-in, but Michael played that autistic man. Shame 'cause he didn't have to physically change and they overlooked Kane. Again.

Kane's character, my character, our character in this film can't find the lake. He looks for it from the moment he drives down the mountain into town. He searches for it all day and night, stays at this guesthouse called The Lakeview, but he can't see it. He goes for a walk to find it but he can't, and all the time he's surrounded by people who have been waterskiing and fishing and paddling about.

There's a boy in a blue cap at the edge of the water watching me.

You get used to it.

> *He looks towards the boy and smiles.*

Bonjour.

> *Back to us.*

This is an independent feature. Low budget, high stakes.

Gina, my agent, says this could be Kane's crossover film, his potential McConaughey moment. This script. This director. It's awards material. There is a scene in this that Gina's excited about. It's going to see us doing some pretty breakthrough stuff.

Rita?

Ricky?

[*To his crew*] Okay.

> *He relaxes.*

They had a class reunion. Wonder if Rabbit went? I didn't go. I should have sent my hands along. People would have recognised them. My hands are more successful than anyone else's entire body.

I checked online for a gym before I came, but the name of the town didn't even come up. No flights go here because there isn't an airport. Kane will probably helicopter in.

I drove. But it's all good—I like driving. Gave me time to plan for Paris—the diet, the workout routine.

[*To his crew*] Again? Okay.

> *He takes the pose.*

I stopped at a gas station on the way and there was this guy there, didn't say a word, but as he filled the tank, I saw his hands. The way the sunlight hit his knuckles and made the grease sparkle. The strength of his squeeze on the pump.

He recognised me. He does that thing men do when they recognise me, keeps trying to look me in the eye. I pay cash instead of credit and say you can get a picture if you want. So he gets his selfie with Kane and I make his day.

I drove down the mountain into town, hit the main street, and then it got really dark. I couldn't see a thing. Just kept hearing this rumble. There must be a waterfall that flows into the lake.

When I finally found the place I'm staying, the light came on on the front porch and there was this little hobbit dwarf thing there. I didn't know what it was, and then its face screwed up and it reached out and shook my hand and said, 'You've arrived. I'm Linda. I'll show you to your room.'

Am I on the wrong set?

Renee?

Kane and me were both rising stars. I was rising to the top of the hand-modelling world and Kane was doing his plays.

Then there was *The Taxidermist*, our first film.

People still do that cat sound at me in the street. Kane didn't cope with the fur, but we clicked. The director said so. Everyone said so. And it's there on screen.

So I stopped hand modelling and after that he gave me this.

    A wristwatch.

Do you like it? Kane did the ads.

The boy in the blue cap's still staring. Must be a *Taxidermist* fan. That's still our biggest film.

He's sure I'm him. Check this out.

[*To the boy*] 'Stuff this, motherfucka. Get out of the pool.'

Kids all love that line.

I'll give him an autograph later. Then I'll find a gym and send Kane a pixt.

Sound travels on water. You hear all sorts of random things out here.

Giggling.

Rumbling.

Silence.

Rowena!

SCENE TWO

SC. 61. EXT. TALIPIA STREET. AFTERNOON.

I have to walk up a street and knock on a door.

> *He walks up the street and knocks on a door.*

[*To his crew*] Slower?

[*To his crew*] Okay.

> *He does it again, slower.*

That's where we're staying, in the guesthouse over there on the hill in front of the mountain.

Yesterday I thought I heard rumbles coming from it. Makes you feel like you are living on the edge of life which is where you need to be if you're an actor. That's what Kane says.

That's why he's been delayed.

He's preparing with Kaftan Maggie, his acting guru.

Kane said I should do some acting classes.

He got me a one-on-one with Kaftan Maggie.

> *He does the walk and knock as he speaks.*

Her studio's covered in headshots of her alumni.

She holds my head in her hands, sniffs the top of my skull, and she whispers yes. Yes.

Kaftan Maggie says, 'Find the snow'. She leaves me in the centre of the room and turns on a fan. She passes me lace and ice and takes my shirt off. 'Find the snow,' she yells. I look for the snow all around the room. 'Look inside yourself!' she shouts.

Kane said it can take some time.

> *He relaxes.*

After we do *The Taxidermist*, Kane and me do *Briefcase Bomb*, *Far Enough Away, Concentration, Briefcase Bomb 2, Close Call,*

Wireless, and then Kane gets cast in *Cain and Abel.* Gina, my agent, says it's a story about twins. Kane says he'll speak to his people but they cast someone else as Abel so that I can play Kane's double again.

[*To his crew*] The gravel under my feet?

[*To his crew*] Okay.

The room they serve breakfast in at the guesthouse looks out at the mountain.

The hobbit, Linda, she's there staring out, clutching a spoon and cracking the eggs like little heads. Mouth full of orange juice and egg yolk she says, 'It's a volcano. Extinct, but I still hear it.'

[*To his crew*] Harder?

[*To his crew*] Yep.

[*To his crew*] With a turn back then?

[*To his crew*] It's all good.

> *He does it again.*

I was thinking the hobbit worked at the guesthouse but then she turned up on location. She watched me all day yesterday. Squinty little eyes peering my way.

[*To his crew*] Not knocking, rapping?

[*To his crew*] Rapping.

> *And once more.*

When we stopped for lunch she was piling her plate in the caterer's tent saying, 'Nice to have a sit-down for lunch', and I'm thinking why are they feeding her?

Then Perry, the second AD, is all smiles next to her asking me, 'Have you met Linda?'

She's chewing beetroot, juice all over her teeth, and staring at me intently. Perry puts his arm around her and says, 'Isn't she magic? Linda Hunt's my lucky charm.'

'I need to find a gym.' I'm on a plan for the Eiffel Tower scene. The climb.

I saw Kane on 'Entertainment Tonight'. They're already promoting *Hall of Mirrors*. He was in short sleeves. His hairy arms. He looks bigger. I left a message about Kane's arms on 'ET' for Gina, my agent. I left one for Kane too.

When I find the gym I'll send him some pics of my arms.

When he gets here we can train together.

After lunch, Linda's still looking at me.

'I'd like to watch you again.' She says.

'I find the stillness very helpful. Your stillness. It's … beautiful.'

Linda likes talking.

She tells me the town has these storms. The mountain acts like some sort of rod for clouds and pressure systems and things … There was a lake tsunami. Water crashed over the town and down the valley and took cows and fish and some girl. They found them all in the valley, the fish still flapping, so they collected them in baskets and brought them all up and put them back in the lake. They have a day to commemorate it every year. Flapping Day. Linda says that's in the script now.

She finds my stillness beautiful. Stillness is one of my things. Kane'll be impressed.

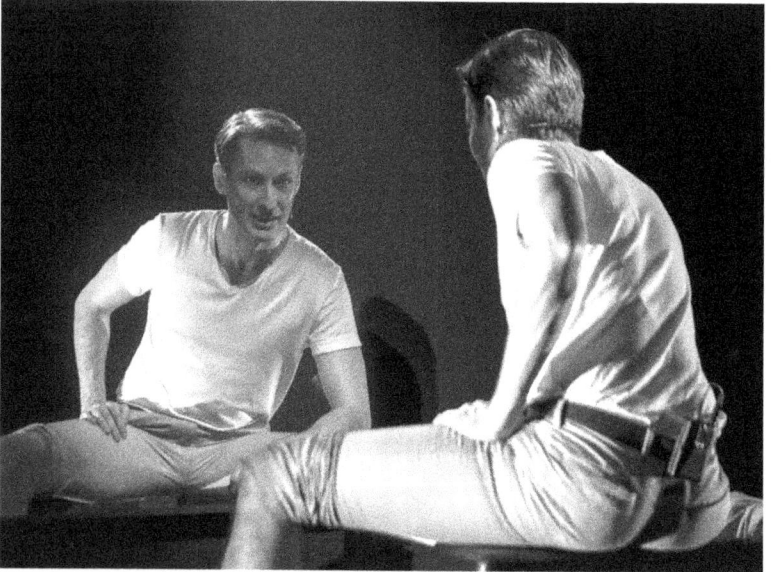

Luke Mullins in the 2016 production of LAKE DISAPPOINTMENT *at the Carriageworks, Sydney. (Photo: James Brown)*

SCENE THREE

SC. 44. INT. THE LAUGHING TROUT DINER. LATE AFTERNOON.

Sometimes they tell you they are going to use bits of you and you go and tell people they are using you, sit in the cinema and go this bit is me, but then it's Kane and you don't know whether to confess or just sit there and pretend as they gasp.

Perry's intern finally showed me where the gym is. It's just under the big plastic fish with the sign in its mouth. There all along.

It's fully equipped with beautiful mirrors. They even have them on the roof. I had the workout of my life. Sixpack. Abs. Pecs. Calves. Clavicles, and then I sent Kane some pics.

I thought I saw Kane today coming out of the tackle shop getting into a pick-up truck. He was too big and he's still in acting lockdown. He'll text me when he's out.

I want to tell him about Linda. I googled her. She must be good. She won an Oscar. She beat Cher. Her acceptance speech is on YouTube and there's a close-up on her hands clutching it … the way the light glints from the statue in her tiny little hands. Wonder where she keeps it? Did she bring it along? Is it in the guesthouse? Only Best Supporting, but perhaps she'd let me hold it?

This film's our chance, Kane's chance.

[*To his crew*] Yes.

They are going to use my hands in this.

  We focus on the DOUBLE*'s hands.*

I've come so far since *Mix It In*. That's where I got my break. The chef was very good with recipes and banter, but he had these monkey hands.

I have better hands than Kane's. And better arms. His are hairy. They often use my feet, everything from the knees down. I've done a lot of butt stuff.

We have the same colour eyes but he has this power with his. When he looks at people it's like he locks onto them and casts a spell. Men, women, dogs, everyone's the same. He can convince them to do anything.

When we did *The Taxidermist* the consultant kept staring at my eyes. She told me she'd never seen a person with eyes like mine before, and when I asked her what she meant, she said, 'Can someone help me move this camel?'

I know Kane so well, but even when I look at rushes it's hard to tell. Is it my neck or his? Who's ankle is that? Our watches and our bodies are in sync. We go to the toilet at the same time. When we first met there was this one time when he finished my sentence.

They've never used my eyes.

> *Another take.*

This film's called *Lake Disappointment*. The same as the town. I don't know which came first. The town, the lake, the film, the disappointment.

The lake was hard to find at first. I told Linda about that and she laughed and said art blurs with reality and reality blurs with art.

She says the director is quite experimental. He's had her doing a *montage*. That's French for collage.

I used to make celebrity collages. Mix up the body parts. Start with John Stammos' head and give him Christian Slater's ears, and Rob Lowe's chest with Corey Haim's legs. I was always really good with scissors.

My teacher said, 'You're dexterous. You can really use your hands.' And then she looked at my hands for such a long time and I kept them so still they could have hypnotised her. I think there was a tear in her eye, and she was about to say something to me, I could see it forming on her lips, and then Rabbit dropped a pot of glue and she had to yell at her instead.

This is a very important scene. It's Kane alone in the diner in the town the day after he arrives.

It sets up a lot of the interior world of character things.

Kane always talks about working out the inner life of a character—

what they're thinking about—their thoughts. How do you film thoughts? How do you know what they are? Anyone could be having any thoughts.

So, I work on the physical shape of the scene, the set-up and the light and the movement, and then he comes in and has his thoughts.

I'll be much busier in Paris. More action, less thoughts. The Eiffel Tower climb, the shootout in *The Hall of Mirrors*. Can't wait for that one.

Linda plays the waitress in this scene. It's actually an operational restaurant at night and during the day they do the catering.

There's a lot of difficult action in this. They need my hands. It's how it works every time. Usually Kane is here and we take it in turns. To inspire each other. But it's all good. I guess they'll just splice it in later.

We did this scene this morning and then Perry said we need do it again, to get it more real.

I was confused by that. I was really moving the cup. But he didn't think it was real. I told Linda when she was refilling my coffee. She listened and just looked at my nose forever and then in this soft voice she asked me, 'What do you want?'

The diet's working. Trainer said don't weigh yourself because it isn't accurate and you have to lose weight before you add bulk. The protein will pay off, the egg whites, the chicken breasts.

Kane has more hair on his arms.

'What do I want?'

Kane's nose is slightly smaller than mine. Make-up always shades out my bridge.

I've thought about surgery.

'What do I want?'

I'm a very positive person. I don't say no. People like a positive person. My favourite phrase is 'It's all good'. I say that all the time.

SCENE FOUR

SC. 37. EXT. THE LAKE SHORE. FOG. EARLY MORNING.
He runs.

This scene will be quick. Just our feet jogging on the sand.

Boy with the blue cap again. 'Stuff this, motherf …' He's gone.

Apparently the lake's a metaphor. Linda thought I should know. It's all surfaces and undertows and ecosystems, and at the end when our character finally finds the lake … he stands at the edge and sees himself in it. Music swirls and that's the big moment. It all clicks into place.

The crew are getting prickly. Things have been a bit tense on set. Nobody has said anything to me, but it must be because Kane's not here yet. He called me this morning, probably to explain, but I could only hear him walking. It's all good.

I went for a run after he called and this photographer came out from behind a tree yelling out our name. She chased me up the street to get photos, but when she got up close she just looked at me and said she was sorry because she thought I was Kane, but it was a silly mistake because up close we look so different. What a fucking idiot.

[*To his crew*] Okay.

　　His action changes.

Even twins have little things about them. Little difference, hairs, moles.

Like those Russian twins we saw at the casino when we were shooting *Path of the Willing*. The way their blond hair shone in chandeliers. They looked so symmetrical. So together. So complete.

The lady beside me whispers they're the Frakandys. Randy and Andy Frakandy.

One of them had a chipped tooth. You can get that fixed but you can't take scars away. The Frakandys win big and leave and then the croupier says, 'You know they do porn? Twincest.'

I'm not sure if was Andy or Randy, but one of Frakandys has a scar on his right hand.

When I worked out last night my shorts felt loose. But I'm stacking and I'm fine. I've eaten eighteen eggs and a chicken, this meatloaf from the diner and some pie, a shake, a burger, steak, fries. I don't need steroids.

SCENE FIVE

SC. 7. INT. CAR. A RAINY. DAY.

He drives.

Things I have found disappointing in my life … not being chosen for the Wobble Bobble ad, being an only child, fireworks, the Dead Sea, *Briefcase Bomb 2* going straight to DVD, being sent to Vanuatu as a decoy when Kane went to the clinic in Tahiti, the day Kane married Mimi, Kane turning down that thriller because Mimi had an eating disorder.

I'm not actually driving this car. They tow it on a trailer. Just lots of shots of the inside of the car, shots of my hands on the wheel, shots of the back of my head, me looking forward, that sort of stuff.

The town's filled up. The guests in the guesthouse have become guests in the film, and customers in the diner don't eat the food anymore, they just wait for the take. Linda is a waitress, but the other waitress is the caterer. And Linda's running the guesthouse now. I saw her behind the counter taking payments and giving keys.

Linda keeps talking about the reveal. I just nod. I never read the script. Kane and Linda both make pencil marks all over the script. I don't get time to make marks on scripts.

Shot of the briefcase. Don't know what's in it.

Files? Some sort of information.

Briefcase Bomb was an action romance with a real bomb. This case hasn't got a bomb inside. They want to get a lot of shots going from Kane to the case. For tension. Like a Stephen King film.

I'm the hands that touch the briefcase. Check this out.

It's important to be very still.

See?

I'm much stiller than Kane.

[*To his crew*] Yep.

He relaxes.

Luke Mullins in the 2016 production of LAKE DISAPPOINTMENT *at the Carriageworks, Sydney. (Photo: James Brown)*

They're washing the car again.

Keep thinking of those hands I saw on the man at the gas station. Maybe I'll stop on the way home and say something. That could really help him, open up his whole world, give him a new start. He could have a very different life. People in entertainment are always giving back.

My hands were in *Briefcase Bomb* for eighty seconds all up.

I sent rushes in to the Body Double Awards. They have body double awards every year at the convention in Atlanta. My still hands on the briefcase were on the long-list for nominations.

In Atlanta, it's just us. We call each other by our actor's names.

Nice to see you, Brad. Jennifer … Jennifer.

It's the only time we can really be ourselves.

No stand-ins, no stunt doubles, 'cause they all come and go. In Atlanta it's just us body doubles because we are the constants.

You're only allowed to come to the convention if you're working.

Poor Heath. So good on horseback. Nobody's seen him.

> *He drives again.*

[*To his crew*] What?

[*To his crew*] Shaking?

[*To his crew*] More like Kane?

Well, it's hardly going to be like Brad or George, is it? Jesus.

[*To his crew*] It's all good.

Wonder if Linda's ever had a double?

If I saw her in the street, I would never have looked at her. I don't think anyone would unless … She just isn't beautiful in any way, so why would you look? But it's a real surprise 'cause when you actually sit with Linda you see she has this thing about her. Kane will see it.

'What do you want?'

I've heard that before.

That night when I stayed in the bar and drank with Ryan at the convention in Atlanta. There was a girl in the booth who was staring at us both and he went right over and said, 'Hey, girl', and she joined us for a few drinks, but we don't recognise her and she says, 'Guess'.

I have no idea where to start, Renée? She laughs.

Jessica, Jennifer, Cameron, Mila, Charlize.

She shakes her head. The next morning she's up on stage in front of us all. She's the keynote speaker, but nobody recognises her and nobody is listening until she pulls Meryl out of the audience and sticks a post-it note on her forehead. She's reading lines from a post-it note on Meryl's forehead and saying that's how a double she won't name has been treated fourteen films in a row.

The convention hall of doubles is still. She stares out at us for ages until she finally says, 'What do you want?'

The catering at the convention is really healthy, for Atlanta. They go to a lot of trouble to make it special … kale sculptures …

[*To his crew*] Yep.

>   *He relaxes.*

Polishing.

Then I'll show them who's Kane.

>   *He drives.*

I was a finalist in a Christmas colouring competition at a shopping mall.

They never said who actually won, but I was the only one who did a collage. The twenty best artists got taken to a chocolate factory as the prize. There were only two boys. I expected a chocolate waterfall.

This marketing executive kept looking at us. And at the end of the production line he said they were shooting an ad and then they picked out James.

They gave James chocolate and took photos of him eating it. I tried to stand close to him in case they changed their mind. They put reflective gold foil screens around so that when the light bounced off James' face it looked glowing and magical. But even without the foil, James had a spark. He became the face of the Wobble Bobble Bar.

I make friends with James, but it is hard to be best friends. All the chocolate gets in the way. He asks me over to his place. But when I get there, there's other boys, teeth brown from all the Wobble Bobble Bars. They laugh every time James speaks, but they just want chocolate, so when they leave, I tell James' mum I thought it was a sleepover and she lets me stay.

James has this amazing fish tank in his room, and while he is watching TV, I look at the fish, ask him which one is his favourite, and he points at the angelfish, but doesn't speak, just pretends he's really into the show, but I know he's just waiting for the Wobble Bobble ad to come on. James waits for his ad all night but it doesn't come on. Finally he falls asleep.

I take the fish out of the tank and watch it breathe.

Then it stops and I put it back.

When James wakes up the next morning he sees it floating dead on the top and bursts into tears.

I made the Wobble Bobble boy cry and even when he's sad he looks beautiful. The tears make this straight line down his cheeks and his eyelashes flutter like little moth wings.

I do this yawn and open my eyes. It's good. Put my arm around his shoulders and I look at myself in the reflection of the fish tank glass while he cries. I'm not blotchy or sad and I don't look special. James sees me in the mirror and stops crying, moves away.

James changes schools and I only see him on TV after that. He makes another Wobble Bobble ad the next summer for the new milky white one. He is wearing this white tracksuit and his teeth sparkle and he looks like he's gotten over the fish.

They make Wobble Bobble Bars in fifty-four flavours now. A little boy who looks like James does the ads.

I saw this TV special where they showed James in the first Wobble Bobble ad. His hair still glinting in the sun. The studio audience clap and James comes out.

He's fatter and he's lost the front of his hair.

The boy who does the ads now skips out and sits on James' lap. They say something at the same time that makes the studio audience laugh.

Mini James tells everyone he likes the salted caramel bacon one best and James smiles, his teeth as white as they always were, looks right into the camera and says, 'I like the original'.

[*To his crew*] Sorry? The way I …

More like Kane. More like Kane.

All good.

More like Kane.

More like Kane.

More like Kane.

Kane. Kane.

SCENE SIX

SC. 104. INT. BATHROOM. LAKEVIEW INN. DUSK.

This is the bathroom scene in the guesthouse with the dripping taps.

They're shooting me from the neck down. Front-on.

So this is it. The big one. The McConaughey. My legs and me and my reflection in the mirrors and the shiny tiles.

Gina, my agent, sent a message this morning. She knows this is important. This scene is the clincher. My body and Kane's thoughts. This is what the Academy voters are looking for.

Kane got here last night, so it's all systems go. I haven't seen him yet but I heard the helicopter.

We have to sit in the bath and block out Linda's character walking up and down the hallway as the tap drips and he goes to another place, a kind of flashback memory which makes a lot of sense when you look at who he is now. Kane's department.

Kane must still be in make-up. He'll be here any minute. Make-up and wardrobe need us both on set so they can match us. Stand us side by side and check that everything is the same, everything lines up.

It's a complicated set-up. The mirrors, the steam, the taps, the towels.

But I'm ready for this. Pumped. Just worked out for three hours. Stacked my protein. Chickens. Eggs. Fish. Feeling good. Feeling huge.

Linda's just outside.

The director's shooting this scene himself. He's on his way … Perry's nervous.

The robe they gave me was baggy. It kept slipping off. Probably just cheap fabric.

There's been a lot of talking. Dripping.

Linda's footsteps again.

Linda whispering on the other side of the door.

It's all good. I'm ready for this. We both are. Water's shrivelling my skin, but I'm focusing on the award.

Footsteps. Different feet now. Kane?

No. The director.

His hair is very serious.

He's whispering as he waves his hands about in the steam. He's shouting for Perry and leading him out. Raised voices in the corridor.

My reflection in the tiles. Leg looks strange. Shrivelled. Runty.

Like the cherries at the lake house where we went on holiday when I was a kid. Cherries way too bitter to eat, they just dropped to the ground and rotted by the water's edge—runty—that's what Dad called them.

I was an only child. Each morning that holiday I wake early to stand at the end of the pier, lake shimmering still, and nothing moves, and I look at myself in the water. Runty.

More steam.

More footsteps. Kane?

No. The director and Perry, looking flustered.

They're wiping the mirrors again.

They're moving them because of the reflection of the cameras.

Taps dripping.

The director isn't speaking to me directly. He's speaking through Perry.

He wants the steam thicker and the tap drip and the footsteps to be in time.

He doesn't look at me either, but they want to get things with the mirrors right. Water's getting really cold.

It's all good.

Director's staring at my leg. Keeps shaking his head and he's whispering to the DOP and I'm not meant to hear, but bathrooms echo, so I hear when he raises his voice and says, 'His leg isn't …'

I look at the refection of my leg in the shimmering tiles.

It's all good.

The water ripples and there's this boy at the edge of the lake by the house, he's smiling some sort of challenge. I tread water, watch him swimming towards me. Then we're face to face and I don't say a word. I can hear him breathing. He looks into my eyes and they look like mine. He laughs. So do I. The laughter's echoing, it's spreading all over the lake.

The boy appears there every day. He comes down a path from over the hill or from under the water. I watch him, he watches me. I copy the way he curls his lip and spits and swears. He splashes my face.

We take Mum's valium, stand in the bathroom, run the bath but forget the water—steam up the room, steam up the mirror, it hides us but when we wipe it away we are revealed. A razor brushes over his finger, blood oozes out the tip, drops, spreads, makes the water rust as I feel the stab of his pain at the tip of mine.

We lie in the strange light of the night while the tap runs. Us on the tiles next to each other, close together.

Your leg touches mine. I feel it first, then look at it in the mirror; your leg and mine, your arm my lips your eyes my heart beating the blue veins on our arms, pulsing together in time.

You twist into me and I twist into you. You find a bruise on my knee like a plum. You make a circle around the fruit and growl, and I bite your leg and your face, bite a chunk out of your cheek and leave the piece of your face hanging, you try to bite me back but I spit your face out on the shiny tiles and push you to the ground. Your face in the mirror. My little smile.

Steam rises around my body and I see your body shivering below.

Hands shaking, blue skin stretched over rib bones poking out, brittle elbow resting on tiles and you looking up at me. I see it and I turn away, a hand wipes the mirror and I see my shrivelled face, the cameraman tries to capture it, tries another angle but no matter what he does the reflection doesn't look right, it won't come up on screen, there's nothing there to catch.

The director's glasses fog up and he hurls his mug across the room. It smashes against the side of the bath and he says, 'Christ all fucking mighty!' but not to me because Perry doesn't repeat it.

The steam has cleared and Kane is not on set.

Everything except the dripping stops.

Perry sighs and covers his face.

The director pulls at his hair and makes this sound, this groaning, and then he points at the mirror, at the reflection of me in the mirror. Perry looks at the mirror.

My thoughts are giving me away.

They turn off the taps, throw the towels on the tiles. Pack up the lights and the cameras.

The director says, 'We cannot use this', and slams the door.

I look at the mirror. There's nothing there.

They cannot use this.

SCENE SEVEN

After the disaster in the bathroom I know I have to find Kane. If I can just see him I'll know what to do with my hands and …

I search the town. Fireworks burst and champagne corks pop. The diner is full of people screaming and laughing, pointing out the window at the sky as it explodes, they don't even see me come in.

Kane?

Kane?

Kane?

Kane?

Kane?

I turn and run into the flashing night. People huddled around a fire by the lake. Kane? I run through the streets and burst into the lobby of some hotel I hadn't seen before, everyone singing, Kane nowhere to be found, the fish with the sign in its gaping mouth, and the boy in the blue cap staring up at the moon and no sign of Kane.

My legs are heavy, so I walk back to the guesthouse, climb the steps, but the key to my room won't turn in the lock. I knock on Linda's door. Music bursts out when she opens it, she's wearing a sparkly red party hat, clutching a flute of champagne and a plate of croissants, she looks at me and blinks and says, 'What do you want?'

I open my mouth but nothing comes out and she slurs the question again, 'What do you want?', and I can't move my lips, so she shrugs and shuts the door.

I go outside, it's already dawn. A crowd has gathered. They seem excited. I try to find Kane in the crowd but none of them look special. They don't notice I'm him. They push in around me and I am trapped, I try to get out but a bus pulls up and we are all schooled on like fish.

The bus toots its horn and we're driving down the mountain.

A mousey woman next to me says, 'Isn't this thrilling? I've been waiting for the Flapping Day scene.'

And he'll be there for the Flapping Day scene?

'Who? Kane? I don't think so. Haven't you done this before?'

But he needs me.

'He's arrived.'

'Arrived?' she says. 'He's been here for weeks!'

I have to get off this bus.

I reach for the red emergency brake handle but my arms feel weak and my legs go like jelly as a woman with a clipboard pushes me back into my seat says, 'Where do you think you're going? We need all you funny-looking extras to be townsfolk for the Flapping Day scene.'

Do you know who I am? Look at me. Think about it—how can I stand in? Who would I be? What if they film me? Who will they think I am if they film me?

But clipboard just turns her back and blocks the aisle and we pick up speed down the mountain.

The extra smiles and says, 'Good try. The lengths people go to see him. I understand why, I mean I thought he looked good in *Briefcase Bomb 2*, but you should see him now. Wow.'

You know it's all good.

Kane didn't …

It's all good.

He needs …

It's all …

And he'll …

All

Bus stops at the bottom

All pushed out

Some guy with a …

Barks orders

A van.

The RSPCA.

Lady with rubber gloves

Fish in a giant truck.

Flapping fish all over the rocks.

A whistle.

People with …

Chase flapping fish.

Someone yelling.

Yelling to me.

To go.

Go!

Grab a fish.

RSPCA

Hurry!

Fish gasping

Gills stop.

Eyes go dull.

Luke Mullins in the 2016 production of LAKE DISAPPOINTMENT *at the Carriageworks, Sydney. (Photo: James Brown)*

SCENE EIGHT

I walked back up the mountain, clutching my fish. It took all day.

When I got there Perry's intern took it back, said, 'They filmed the last scene yesterday in the valley. It's a wrap. That's why they had the fireworks, Kane's gone.'

I follow her across the set, the town, into a parking lot, but I'm having trouble keeping up with her. What about continuity? What about my hands and my arms? How can Kane be gone?

I go to Perry's tent, I bang on the flap but the tent falls down.

The diner's lost its sign. Tables and chairs all stacked up in the parking lot.

The bait shop walls are stacked in a pile.

They're carrying the weights from the gym to a truck.

The fish with the sign in its mouth is in pieces on the back of another truck, its engine roars and it drives up the hill.

A shape on the grass where the guesthouse was.

No sign of anyone.

Kane?

I see the boy in the blue cap ducking down a little path. I try to follow him but he disappears behind a tree. His footprints end in the damp soil at the edge of the lake.

Everything's rumbling?

A shiny thing glints and moves. A fish?

It's spinning round and round.

It's coming to me, it brushes my leg.

A Wobble Bobble wrapper. It floats on the surface of the water and sinks into the mud below.

The lake bubbles. The water, the mud, the wrapper all being sucked away.

If they have not already, the house lights should come on. He should be left there for as long as possible.

THE END

PLAYS BY CURRENCY PRESS

Silent Disco
Lachlan Philpott

Tamara and Jasyn are in love. Jasyn lives with Aunty and his brother Dane is in prison for dealing. Jasyn wants to take Tamara to the formal, but he hasn't got the cash. In a world of absent mothers and missing fathers, Mrs Petchall battles to keep another year of students out of the ranks of the vanished. Winner of the Griffin Award (2009) and an AWGIE Award (2012).

978-0-86819-961-0, also available as an ebook

Truck Stop
Lachlan Philpott

Sam and Kelly live out west. They spend their lives waiting for texts, for boyfriends and those bitches in Year Ten to leave school so they can have somewhere decent to hang. Bored one recess, the girls escape through the hole in the fence. Hang out at the truck stop on the highway. When a truck pulls up, Sam issues Kelly a dare. Winner of an AWGIE Award (2013).

978-1-92500-518-9, also available as an ebook

Michael Swordfish
Lachlan Philpott

Who is Michael Swordfish? And who knows where he's gone? For two years award-winning playwright Lachlan Philpott collaborated with students from Newington College, Sydney, to bring their voices and worlds to life. *Michael Swordfish* is the exciting product of this collaboration: a play that traverses the tumultuous landscape of the teenage experience with a sober truth and darkly comic voice.

978-1-76062-083-7, also available as an ebook

Holding the Man
Tommy Murphy

Based on Timothy Conigrave's celebrated memoir of the same name, which won the 1995 UN Human Rights Award for Non-Fiction and was voted one of Australia's top 100 most favourite books. Tommy Murphy's stage adaptation faithfully captures the book's heart-wrenchingly honest portrayal of a fifteen-year relationship, but also succeeds in transforming it into a unique theatrical experience. Winner of the NSW Premier's Literary Award (2007), the Philip Parsons Young Playwright's Award (2007, and an AWGIE Award (2007). Published in a double volume with *Strangers in Between*.

978-0-86819-796-8, also available as an ebook

A Rabbit for Kim Jong-il
Kit Brookman

Johann's super-sized rabbits are his pride and joy. Much to his surprise, the Supreme Leader of the Democratic People's Republic of Korea has taken a special interest, and will stop at nothing to get his hands on them. When a bungled undercover rescue mission transports Johann to North Korea, he finds himself, and the bunnies he betrayed, in a bit of a stew. Preposterously based on a true story.

978-1-92500-548-6, also available as an ebook

Angela's Kitchen
Paul Capsis

In 1948, Angela left Malta. Her destination: Australia. In Surry Hills, she could build a bright new life. Back in Malta, a young man with flowing black hair has returned to claim his past. Paul Capsis is walking home. A journey that begins at a kitchen table becomes a sprawling family history and a fitting tribute to a much-loved matriarch. Winner of the Helpmann Award for Best New Australian Work (2012).

978-0-86819-946-7, also available as an ebook

Sappho ... in 9 Fragments
Jane Montgomery Griffiths

Inspiration, abomination, lesbian pin-up, Christian tear-up, Roman's reference, Egyptians' refuse, empty vessel, imaginative void... 2700 years ago, Sappho was the world's first love poet and the tenth muse of the Ancient Greeks. Placed alongside a modern love story of sensuality, sexual awakening and broken hearts. Shortlisted for the NSW and Victorian Premier's Literary Awards (2011).

978-0-86819-886-6, also available as an ebook

As Told By the Boys Who Fed Me Apples
R. Johns

Sandy was the only Australian War Horse to return home from World War I. This is his poignant and fragmented war story. Through Sandy we experience the lives of three men who fought in the war. Each is affected by their symbiotic relationship with the horse. This unique, poetic piece of theatre captures the brutality of war and the heroism of the soldiers and horses who served.

978-1-76062-052-3, also available as an ebook

Not in the Script
John McCallum and Jenny Nicholls

This monologue collection offers up a challenge: to perform with voices that aren't from play scripts. These pieces are a fresh and sharp source of material for performance, auditions and workshops. The characters range from lovers in the King James Bible to a sci-fi Artificial Intelligence unit navigating gender identities between planets. Classic sources include *Great Expectations, Jane Eyre, Ulysses* and *The Bell Jar* and work from Beckett, Kafka and Mark Twain. Strong contemporary monologues come from work by Raymond Carver, Miranda July, Elena Ferrante, Jeffrey Eugenides, Alice Munro and David Sedaris. Australian voices speak in iconic moments from *Jasper Jones* and John Marsden's *Tomorrow* series and from definitive work by David Malouf, Elizabeth Jolley, Geraldine Brooks, Morris Gleitzman, Jeanine Leane, Gayle Kennedy and Alice Pung.

978-1-92500-583-7, also available as an ebook

www.currency.com.au

Visit Currency Press' website now to:

- Buy your books online
- Browse through our full list of titles, from plays to screenplays, books on theatre, film and music, and more
- Choose a play for your school or amateur performance group by cast size and gender
- Obtain information about performance rights
- Find out about theatre productions and other performing arts news across Australia
- For students, read our study guides
- For teachers, access syllabus and other relevant information
- Sign up for our email newsletter

The performing arts publisher